To Reign

From
John Michael Bradley

Future Leaders or Losers:
Guidelines for Understanding Youths

John Michael Bradley

WIPF & STOCK · Eugene, Oregon

Resource Publications
A division of Wipf and Stock Publishers
199 W 8th Ave, Suite 3
Eugene, OR 97401

Future Leaders or Losers
Guidelines for Understanding Youths
By Bradley, John M.
Copyright©2005 by Bradley, John M.
ISBN 13: 978-1-5326-6065-8
Publication date 6/13/2018
Previously published by PublishAmerica, 2005

"*Future Leaders or Losers* is an excellent tool for parents and all adults who deal with youths today. John Bradley's commonsense approach in dealing with today's youths will assist adults in not only understanding what youths today are dealing with, but positive ways to impact that youth's life to make him/her the best individual they can be."

—Christian Jensen
Gang Specialist, Elgin Police Department

Table of Contents

Introduction

The purpose of this book is to be a little more simple regarding youth problems and solutions to those problems. It seems that parents and caretakers raising children and dealing with the problems of youths and juveniles practically have to enroll in college or be at that intellectual level to not only get the material, but understand the content as well, for personal application. My approach focuses on being able to understand the contents whether one has an 8th grade education, or a high school diploma. However, it should have an appeal to anyone who has the intellect and has entered higher education, or who is at that level. Therefore, my attempt has been to include generally anyone who can read, whether they are in or going to college or not, but not to undermine anyone regardless of the level they're at.

As an adult male, I have and continue to wear several so-called hats, being a father, a son, a grandfather, a brother, youth counselor, social service worker, mental health professional, case manager, caseworker and so on. For more than 30 years, I have attempted to get across to parents some understanding regarding the problems associated with growing up as a child and being a juvenile going through its turbulent changes. I found even more valuable information is understanding my own childhood and how difficult it could have been, in spite of how difficult it was. Because of this, I find it very difficult to forget and lose sight of what it's like. My education and professional experiences have enhanced those personal experiences to a point of allowing me to be creative and a little different in dealing with today's youths. Putting it all together requires being and/or working in some of the worst neighborhoods in the country, whether it be Roxbury, Los Angeles, or

Chicago. I feel a sense, or should I say, the *need* to put in writing some necessary information that could possibly help someone somewhere to not only understand what's happening with today's youths' so-called growing pains, but what we can do to help them and ourselves.

This is a simple, relatively easy-to-read guideline on understanding youths and teenagers, and how to apply that understanding in assisting parents and caretakers with guiding them in positive directions. The application of this guidance can be utilized over many years because of stages youths have experienced and will continue to go through for many more years, regardless of the changes in our society. It also can be helpful in numerous cultures around the world because youths and teenagers in every family, culture and country have and will experience the adolescent period of growing up. Although customs and family traditions may differ, the element that remains the same is the hormonal changes youths go through between 12 and 17 years of age. This is a fact of life from a psychological and physical standpoint. No relatively normal individual has or will escape the challenges involved, no matter what tribal, rural, or urban environmental background and orientation is experienced.

Chapter 1

Youths and Juveniles

Other than the period of growth from birth through around 6 years of age, there is no other time during the life cycle where a person goes through such a natural mandatory mental change than the period from 12 to around 17 years of age. It is during this time a person's identity is in the search mode. This is a time turmoil is likely to magnify itself in behavior problems. It's a time where leaders can be recognized, but at the same time, a leader can be lost, more often than not for the rest of their lives. It's a time when understanding and guidance is so important; the person going through this period may not realize themselves what they are doing, and may not know how to handle what they are going through. Although help is very much needed for a constructive journey through this time, help is often destructive in ways such as power plays, psychological standoffs, dictatorship disciplinary approaches, and many times just down right physical and/ or emotional abuse.

What's interesting is for many years, these methods were constructive because the youth in this stage generally did what they were told and had a sense of "hell to pay" if they questioned or had questions about how they were treated and why. In today's society, they generally, and I mean *generally*, don't work. Although it could be said children, youth and juvenile rights have changed and improved, advocacy for this period of growth has increased and been effective. The fact of the matter is, the consciousness of our youths has been raised to the point where the "Do as I say, don't do as I do" rule of parenting does not work anymore. In essence, it is a probability we will never return to this method, given our youths are growing up faster, learning earlier, becoming aware sooner, and developing physically bigger and better. The consciousness today's youths have been raised to will undoubtedly go higher. As caretakers of these youths, we will need to raise the bar and change the approach of our parenting, adjusting our understanding to view all of these changes as positive, and exercise our roles in positive approaches.

During those pre-teen and teenage years, it is one of the most vulnerable growth periods an individual goes through, being receptive to confusion, misunderstanding, misguidance, ignorance, and a host of many emotional challenges and changes. What makes this growing stage unique is the vulnerability is, in a sense, self-guided. In other words, this is the time their decision making is, or can be, based on incorrect advice, bad information, and overall inadequate environmental influences. Although the youth knows right from wrong and knows exactly what they are doing, they are vulnerable and this can cause deadly results. It is the time that is the most dangerous to self-destruction, possibly resulting in life or death situations for that youth and/or members of our society. Although the emotional and hormonal changes contribute to the decision-making, the behavior and deeds involved are done purposely.

Chapter 2

Peer Pressure

During the pre-adolescence and adolescence years, peer pressure is the most influential and vulnerable time to be lead, or the potential to be lead astray. It is the most dangerous times in that it is the time youths actually make the decisions to do the behavior which will/could cost themselves or someone else their life. It is a time that one is likely to literally play Russian roulette with a loaded gun because of the fear of being called and labeled chicken. The need to belong is so great, it is almost as if they cannot live without fitting in.

(In fact, worldwide, teenage suicide is higher than any other age group combined, many with the basis of being unable to cope with what friends, society or family think or will think of them.) It is during this time that peer pressure causes what parents and caretakers call making stupid decisions, being at the wrong place at the wrong time, or just being plain stupid. It's the time one is likely to be a runaway and participate in life's wild side. In other words, being or living on the streets and being vulnerable to the dangers of predators. It is during this time that peer pressure is likely to be instrumental in suicides or suicidal behavior. It is interesting to note all these choices are made by the individual youth, who is actually of sound mind, given the growth circumstances and mindset of this period of time.

Let's look at the positives of peer pressure for a moment. Because of the vulnerability during this time, if peers were participating in positive behavior it is not only likely, but almost a given, that youths hanging around that group will probably be affected because of a need to fit in. Therefore, during this time they are likely to display positive behavior because of peer pressure. It is the time of positive creativity because of that pressure. It is a time one may exercise humanitarian behavior because of the group. Gifted youths feed on each other's gifts and talents, particularly during this peer pressure stage. Although many youths during this time are likely to be labeled a nerd, it usually indicates that person or group is not involved with negative riff-raff. This is all right because that youth has made the choice to not do "stupid behavior," both because of peer pressure, and in spite of it. Many times leaders are evident and, because of positive pressure, attributes are cultivated.

It is very important to understand the magnitude of peer pressure as parents and caretakers. We often don't realize how powerful it is. Many of us feel our youths can withstand it or resist with no problem, but they can't. In actuality, it's a necessary part of the growth cycle. The peers in this stage are an important part of that youth needing to belong, but most importantly, finding their identity and direction. As parents and caretakers, we have to understand our children's characters and help them to select a positive group that allows positive peer pressure. Generally this means starting the process when they are toddlers. However, it can be done when the individual starts the pre-adolescent period. In essence, it's like attempting to select their friends. There is nothing wrong with that, within reason, if we have gotten the youth to be receptive to be around the peers who match their positive character. But parents and caretakers need to know what that positive character is, to match it both with their own youth, and with the individual or individuals that youth will be hanging around.

It is very important for us to take the necessary steps not only to understand how lethal peer pressure can be, but how positive it should be. More times than not, our youth's very lives may depend on it.

In recognizing peer pressure is very important and significant, the parent needs to realize the influence, and adopt a parenting style that circumvents the negatives associated with that pressure. In actuality, there is nothing that can be done about peer pressure because it's simply going to be there. However, the best time to have input in the guidance of the positive selection of peers is before pre-adolescence, specifically as children or toddlers. In other words, at a very early age. It is during these early years that parents more often than not have a monopoly incorporating friends into the child's life. Many times it is during these stages that parents feel it's safe to allow the child to play and be with anyone their age, regardless of the behavior displayed and personally observed by that parent. This is often done without much interference or even supervision. However, it is a most critical period and normally has the least resistance from the child when picking their playmates.

I recall an incident when my 29-year-old daughter was about 3 years old and was outside playing with the next-door neighbor's child, who was the same age. My daughter mentioned later that evening when she was in the house that the little girl told her not to play or talk to another little girl their age because she was white. My daughter really didn't know what she meant, nor understood why she said it. It was explained to her the best it could that there was no difference with children and not to make a difference on how light or dark someone's skin color was. However, that was the last time she played with the other little girl. My daughter was used to being around all types of children of various colors, cultures and backgrounds. At this early age, my daughter didn't have even a remote problem with not playing with that girl next door. It simply didn't make a difference to her, especially since she had other children to play with who shared her approach to picking friends to be with. At 29 years old, neither she nor her children show any difference with their interacting and associating with people.

As parents, we chose to circumvent the negative influence that involved eliminating a component of negative influence. However, we had to be very observant and able to recognize what we felt was incompatible behavior, plus provide guidance and take the necessary actions. It would have been quite a different outcome had we started this type of guidance and correction if she was around 12 or 13 years of age. It most likely would have resulted in hostility and some degree of resistance, to say the least.

This example is typical of the influence parents have early versus later as teens. It can, or should, be generalized to include a constant awareness of negative influences and directions from potential peers and those pressures.

Chapter 3

Gangs as Family

This is a situation that is disturbing, at best. It is unfortunate gangs are considered family to those who join them. It gives a sense of belonging. It commands a sense of responsibility. It portrays a sense of nurturing and develops a sense of pride associated with deeds and behavior. The foundation is primarily its home; in other words, its turf, territory and neighborhood. The structure always has a leader and a second in command, with a similarity to the strong father figure in a family. The primary purpose is to lead, expand, teach, and have solidarity. There's always a financial or money intake operation to operate and pay for expenses and the overall operation of the group. Like the conventional family, it's difficult to disown, get out, or disassociate from, even if from within. There are fights and discord. Like families, gangs protect the members from outsiders. The accomplishments of individuals associated with the group, reflect on the group; misdeeds embarrass the group. Gangs, or the basic formulation of gangs, started more than 150 years ago because of youths hanging out on the streets. Many of these youths had either no family, a partial family (one parent), a family with little substance for influence, or little or no supervision from the family. They started because youths needing to belong created a neighborhood household to fulfill that need. Gangs provide a system to incorporate the things that are needed for the individuals involved that they were missing in their own families. In essence, gangs are simply a substitute for the conventional family structure. It's possible to perceive as an extension, but its influence and power, by far, outweighs the family we feel should be the primary nurturing system our youths are involved in. For more than a century and a half, gangs have been competitive with conventional family and have won many battles and claimed many lives.

What can we do to win the war? How do we direct and put our youths back on the right path? We first need to understand and identify that youths go through many changes, mentally and physically. These are often changes we adults have already gone through, but failed to recall how difficult it is. We need to realize our youths need us to listen, to hear what is said and not said. As parents and caretakers, we have to create the kind of home environment that circumvents and successfully rivals gang life. We have to establish a positive peer group for them to be involved in, to supply directions and values while the child is still young so that when the child becomes a juvenile they will feel gangs have no place in their life. Guide them to the type of people and individuals who will be compatible with non-gang involvement. If that need to belong was fulfilled in the home and by the conventional family, gang involvement and participation would be almost non-existent. However, considering what gangs have evolved into presently, I'm sure there are many parents who rightfully feel that winning this battle, or redirecting one from gangs, is easier said than done. In today's society, gangs are more powerful. They are larger in group size, and not only more competitive with the family structure, but a threat to the family as well. Unlike the family structure, which may have various degrees of positive influence depending on the individual family, overall, or generally speaking, there are no positive gangs. They have various degrees of negative influence instead. Basically, it is a destructive and dysfunctional cancer in our society, which threatens the very purpose of the family system, and it has expanded worldwide.

It is vital we understand the seriousness involved and what we are up against. However, the family system must be not only preserved, but improved also, to ensure its continued survival.

Chapter 4

Everyone, No Matter Who, Has Some Kind of Talent (How to Exploit It)

During the pre-adolescent and adolescent years, individuals often indicate and show clues of talents and gifts they have. As parents and caretakers, we often misinterpret valuable clues displayed by some of the characters and personalities of our youths. Sometimes those clues are more evident than others, such as being able to draw very well, or an unusual ability to learn, read, remember things, or speak well in front of crowds of people, fixing things, building structures, singing, dancing, or even writing well, all at a very young age. However, there are others, which may not be as evident, such as being bossy, that could indicate a strong personality and leadership ability if channeled in a positive direction; having the ability to persuade or attempt to explain everything at an unusual age, which could indicate a gift of having a logical mindset for occupations utilizing logical foundations; an unusual ability for detail awareness, which may indicate the usage of a wider portion of the brain power than the normal person; an almost unbelievable ability as a youngster to talk, speak, or be a speaker, which could indicate a future orator or public speaker, or determination

19

which may almost frustrate a parent, but if developed in a positive direction could almost guarantee success in any occupational field. There are many of these clues we simply don't recognize and, because of our own misunderstanding, or simply not understanding, we wrongly exercise our parenting power to unwittingly discourage their proper development. At times we actually seem to look at these clues as inconveniences and become annoyed at their expressions.

What we can and should do is make a point to examine our youth's characters and unusual behaviors. Try to think of how this particular annoying behavior or character trait can be helpful and fit in society in a positive way. Try to come up with an activity that actually utilizes the behavior in a positive and helpful manner. Instead of being discouraging, encourage seemingly negative and annoying behavior into positive activities. Create or think of some type of activity that would allow the bossy character to be used for positive energy. Put them in charge of something appropriate. Find positive situations the persuading and ever-explaining character can soar in. There is always some contribution that can be made in a positive manner from those misunderstood and seemingly annoying behaviors. We just need to be patient and creative enough to find and realize what they are.

It has been mentioned numerous times and realized by many that our children or youths are the future world leaders, inventors and scientists, or overall "world changers," so to speak. As parents, we tend to think of those world changers coming from someone else's family or a special or different environment then ours. Many of us may not think of it at all, even when we are noticing unusual talent and/or behavior our own child has. If we live in an environment that is at risk for all who live in it and presents numerous negative attributes and challenges, it makes it more difficult to believe your child is special enough to make a positive impact in society. Overall, this mindset and approach has to be changed. As parents, we need to allow ourselves to be believers that we may have a future leader, someone in our family who has what it takes to change something and/or someone in our society for the better. Rather, it's a talent, gift, or an unusual ability to do something different or better than the average person. It is there in that youth to be developed and shared with all of us.

When we look at people like Oprah Winfrey, Bill Gates, Jr., Michael Jordan, Sam Walton (who started Wal-Mart), Henry Aaron, Sammy Sosa, Albert Einstein, Harry Truman (the only president with no more than a high school diploma), Celine Dion (a world-renowned singer), Denzel Washington, and numerous other well-known individuals, we see that all had something special and different about them when they were in their youth. Some of these individuals had parents who didn't have the slightest idea of how big and influential their child would be in our society. They just did what it took to allow them to develop that difference, even if it was an unusual amount of determination to succeed, as was the case with Sammy Sosa.

> *When I was in my teens, I recall having this character trait of always trying to point out some angle to a situation and attempting to get another side of a problem or situation from my mother by asking questions, all the time. It annoyed her quite a bit. However, she didn't stop me from doing so. When I realized what the field of psychology was, I felt, even as a teen, it fit my personality. I eventually went on to receive a BA in applied behavioral science, while taking a natural liking to the fields of social services, mental health and counseling.*

Parents and caretakers are that bridge for youths to develop and utilize their personalities and cultivate their unique characters for positive directions. All youths have a talent, gift and/or a positive contribution to make to society. Look closely at your child, that teenager. You just have to find a way to allow them to put everything in prospective for future productivity.

Chapter 5

Street Psychology vs. Academic Psychology

Street sense, or being streetwise, is what street psychology is. It's a valuable component to survival for youths at risk, and a good tool to use for positive directions in education and academic achievement. Academic psychology is an educational approach with the mindset to use as a means for survival for future reference. Therefore, street psychology is to utilize street knowledge for survival now or in the present, where academic psychology is to utilize that technical education now for better utilization and survival later.

Generally, youths who grow up in challenging environments and are able to be placed in situations where they can receive higher education leading to academic achievement can be a powerhouse in society. We often underestimate the valuable experience of growing up as a youth while living in a disadvantaged environment. Although many times it's one we purposely chose, it can be used to our advantage and importantly to the advantage of our youths. This type of exposure allows a special understanding about hardships and gives invaluable personal insights an individual cannot learn in school and in the books. We can get this across further by informing our youths about our own hardships and experiences, tell them about other family members' trials and tribulations, whether it's about their grandparents, uncles, aunts, or cousins. Try to make a point to relate those challenging experiences to what that youth wants to do or be in the future. Think of someone somewhere in the family who has risen above all odds and has a position in employment, which is positive. If parents and caretakers can generally get this across to youths with understanding and not attempt to compare them to those individuals who have made it out of the environment, it is most likely to make a lasting impression to spark positive result. Street psychology and academic psychology can, and should, go hand in hand.

In learning and exercising street psychology, it is often possible to do without education. However, the activities involved with doing both learning and exercising tend to overlap and sometimes include some form of illegal or immoral deed. Youth exposure usually comes at an early age, quite often before pre-adolescence. They make observation of behavior, deeds and process information for survival physically and psychologically in that environment or one similar to it. The valuable application of this learning process comes when and if that youth takes what they learned and is either guided by someone, or realizes themselves how to use those survival techniques to be legitimately productive and go in positive directions.

Examples include: *learning to recognize when someone is trying to talk you into or out of doing something by lying, and being able to pick that up as its happening; learning to pick up non-verbal communication to detect if someone is afraid, about to cause harm via a fight, or about to take flight; if someone is being sincere or if someone is not interested in what is being said to them.*

There are other behaviors learned from the environment that give clues about being at risk of physical and/or emotional harm before it takes place, learning to carry oneself so others will not detect fear, giving or displaying a sense of confidence to assure predators avoid you, and so on.

These behaviors and more can be learned from the streets, but can be transformed into valuable assets and insights for the preparation to almost any occupation that exist. These and many more are street psychology-based skills. They can usually be learned without books or going to any classroom. They are skills that realistically prepare the individual for survival. However, imagine learning these skills well as a youth and applying them to professions such as being an attorney, a police officer, a social worker, a counselor, or any job where interacting with people is involved. The value would be immeasurable. Coupled with education, that individual is likely to be invaluable to our society as a whole.

Chapter 6

Environment—How it Affects

1. If it Needs Improvement Overwhelmingly, One May Have to Leave it Behind

The environment has a very important part to play in the directions our youths go in. The influence should not be underplayed or underestimated. Its effect will be apparent and realized one way or another, whether it's good or bad. There is no neutral affect for anyone, especially youths. Even if an individual, a youth, or a family's decision is to try as much as possible to stay inside the home and out of the surrounding environment, a neutral position is not taken because a decision has been made to avoid possible circumstances that may happen.

If the environment or neighborhood is too challenging, it may actually be a hazard to one's health, a safety risk by just living there. When the overall influence is overwhelmingly negative, steps may have to be taken to find other alternatives. Consider an environment that is gang infested, full of drug activity, very violence oriented with the type of so-called role models who are consistently going to jail or prison, and the likelihood of changing that neighborhood during that youth's stage of pre-adolescence and adolescence is very unlikely, at best. What do you do? Two words, GET OUT! Obviously, it's not as easy as that, but a serious approach should be taken to move, since you will not be able to change it. What do you do if it's economically impossible? If you live in federal subsidized housing, locate to another housing area that is safer, or get your name on a list by contacting social service agencies, which assist with finding housing. If you live in a home or an apartment where you pay the market or conventional rent, you can still contact agencies that assist in finding housing, but you should be able to get the monies together by making economic sacrifices, for a safer environment. If you set your mind on moving and realize it's the right and safest thing to do, doors will open and the opportunity will come to you. The key ingredient is setting your mind to making it a reality.

2. Send the Youth Away Permanently to Relatives in Other Cities or States

Another solution to coping with a challenging environment you cannot change and is a safety risk, would be to transfer or move the youth or youths, who are likely to be at risk staying there. There are always numerous parents and caretakers who cannot or will not move, for whatever reason. In these cases, find a safe place for the youth to live. As outrageous as this may sound, it's actually a very good move, and one that could very well be the best decision you will ever make in the youth's life, possibly even saving their life. With many of us having relatives in many different places, there is likely to be several relatives living somewhere that is safer and healthier. The considerations need not be limited to just the other side of town. All possibilities should be looked at, whether they're in another city or state. These options could be uncles, aunts, older siblings who are responsible enough, grandparents, godparents, or some other living situations, even with good friends. However, when or if this move is made, the mindset should be that the youth will be in that safer environment and home setting for the remainder of their adolescent years. Placing them for that entire period is much more beneficial then having them spend a summer or a little longer, because it gives the youth some stability and allows them to concentrate on positive directions they are likely to be exposed to. This may seem like a drastic step, but if the parent really focuses on the welfare of the youth and not on how much they will miss them or the need to prove they are a good parent, the overall result should be a very positive one.

While growing up as a teenager, my life was full of experiences that I learned later to use for positive growth as an adult. In reflection on that period in my life, I realized many of those experiences and that environment had a basis for the state of mind I'm in today. My approach to people, my outlook on society in general, and my morals all are interrelated to that time.

My mother, who was a single parent, believed in teaching responsibility. I was the oldest of five children and at one point we had two cousins living with us, making it seven children in the home with one parent. I, along with two sisters, two brothers, and two cousins, were more than encouraged to iron clothes, mop floors, wash dishes and keep the house orderly and clean. They were mandatory chores. I was grown before I appreciated the responsibility I learned then, because as an adult male I knew how to clean house and care for myself. Therefore, it taught me how to be independent early.

I grew up on the west side of Chicago in one of the city's worst neighborhoods in the projects. My friends were all from single parent homes and there were many things to get into. I believe we all dropped out of school by the age of 16 and started hanging out during the day and drinking liquor and partying at night. At one time I even sold marijuana. I also watched a number of teens my age shoot up heroin. I remember a schoolmate being killed playing Russian roulette with a gun, and a few others who were killed in gang fights. My friends and I eventually formed our own gangs, but did it for our own protection. We didn't start trouble, but did retaliate if one of us was harassed or beaten up. Unknown to my mother, I kept a .38 special handgun at my house. It was our gang's gun and wasn't likely to be found at my house.

I was a fast talker, a con man, so to speak. I could talk someone out of almost anything. I could make someone mad enough to the point they felt like hitting me, and then talk them out of doing that. I used logic or what I called street logic, in that I seemed to make sense enough for whomever I was talking to, to think about what I was saying and comply with whatever I wanted them to do. My friends called me the brain of the group. Although I was the youngest of our group or gang, I was always perceived to be the oldest by outsiders. Even though I could fight very well, I didn't like to. I always wanted to reason my way out of a confrontation. At about 17 years old, I realized this environment was hazardous to my health. At one point I almost shot up heroin because friends were doing it, but they ran out of the supply they had just as I got the nerve to do it. I never reached that vulnerability again; I was able to talk myself out of it.

Friends were stealing cars to go joy riding. A couple of times I participated in armed robberies. I had been shot at and chased by rival gangs. To get high, I was sniffing glue, popping pills, drinking lots of alcohol, smoking marijuana, and even drinking cough syrup. It was a dangerous life and environment and I felt I had to get out if I wanted to survive. I also felt like I was caged in.

I soon began to focus on an identity, something more than being a gang member. I began to listen to Aldridge Cleaver of the Black Panther Party. He was the minister of information for the party and was a very good speaker. He was radical, but I felt the party itself was too confrontational and violently oriented for me, so I didn't join. I saw another situation that caught my attention and impressed me. One of my friends had a brother who was in college at the time. He was attending the University of Illinois at Chicago's Circle campus. He received a scholarship to go to Harvard University in Boston, Massachusetts, and eventually finished there with a masters degree. Since he was a black man from my neighborhood, this gave me a tremendous amount of inspiration and incentive to leave the environment I was used to living in.

At the age of 18, I joined the Job Corp program and not only left the neighborhood, but the state as well. It was a great feeling and I felt I was lucky. I hadn't been to jail like every single one of my friends had, and was determined to keep it that way. I had learned by this time, in order to be jail-free, I had to put myself around the type of people, situations and environment where it was less likely to happen.

I learned to use that environment and many of those past experiences for positive growth as an adult. When I think back to my slick con man, fast-talking days, I think of how much it affected the last 30 years or so of my life. I learned the energy put into those early years was best served in my adult years by possibly talking people into doing what was best for them. I learned and found many people who didn't quite know what was best for them, especially youths. Sometimes they became their own stumbling block. I have used my early experience of raw skills, along with my education, to practically talk some of these people out of being in this frame of mind.

I've spent more than 20 years working with youths and don't recall any of the hundreds I've worked with coming from an environment any worse than the one I came from. Because of that background, many of these youths I worked with found it difficult, if not impossible, to manipulate or con me. At the same time, I had sort of a personal identification with them and had an understanding of their situation, background and environment that allowed many to admire and look up to me.

31

I constantly reflect back to my teenage years. Being the age I am now, I can't image what psychological state of mind I would be in if I hadn't gone through those things, but I also think of what things would be like if I hadn't gotten out. Out of the 8 guys I hung out with, only 3 of us made it to our 30th birthday. I do believe because of that time, I chose the field of psychology as my major in college. I was very analytical then, but wasn't aware of the term of what I was doing until I was an adult. I was always asking questions and trying to figure out what someone was going to do, and how and why they were going to do it. I was in my 20s when I realized psychology actually fit the way I was mentally. That environment also enhanced my education and continues to do so, up to the present time. The numerous psychology and sociology courses I've taken basically gave me much insight and understanding of myself and how to further use that early period to continue my quest for additional insight. I find, even now, I have a very difficult time in looking at people's problems, situations and circumstances from just one angle. I find myself so open-minded that at times it even baffles me. I learned to be sympathetic toward people with similar backgrounds I had, which in turn seemed to have generalized over the years to people from any and all cultural backgrounds.

Yes, there is no question that period in my life had and is still having an affect on my adult life. For the most part it's a positive affect. Those experiences of my early years are never forgotten, and seem to have also made a profound engraving and mark on the shape of my overall character as an adult.

As stated earlier, the affects of the environment will be apparent and realized one way or another, good or bad, negative or positive. Although I considered myself lucky, there are many youths out there who are destined to be just as lucky to not only positively affect themselves individually, but the environment and society collectively.

Chapter 7

What Parents Forget
(They Were Once Teens)

All of us adults have gone through pre-adolescence and the adolescent period of growth. Some of us had some difficult times, while others may not have had it as hard. Either way, for all of us, it was a rebellious, challenging and thought-provoking time. We remember what it was like for us, how difficult it was, and how our parents didn't understand and failed to relate to our behavior. However, many of us, as parents, are unwilling to truly apply those experiences we had to *our* children's present state of mind. It is as if we have forgotten how difficult it was to cope with sibling rivalry, peer pressure, parents' expectations, power struggles with parents and within the family, the need to express feelings, trying not to talk back to our parents because we were starting to "feel our oats," and numerous other mental and physical changes we experienced. We forgot how easy it was to be with the wrong crowd because of the need to belong. We forgot how difficult it was to take advice from our parents at face value when their behavior contradicted what they told us how we should behave. We forgot how easy it was to lie about where we've been, or where we were going, to keep from getting in trouble. We forgot how difficult it was to take our parents disciplining us in front of our friends. We forgot how embarrassing it was and how easy it was to talk back because of it. We forgot how easy it was for us to be verbally and/or physically abusive to parents who were being abused one way or another by the other parent or companion. We forgot how difficult it was to respect our parents when they were disrespectful to us as an individual and human being, regardless of our age. We forgot how easy it was for our parents to tell us we were wrong and how difficult it was for them to admit they were. We forgot how difficult it was to tell our parents they were not telling the truth. We forgot how easy it was for us to obtain knowledge about things that wasn't available to them. We forgot how difficult it was for them to except things that we knew, but they didn't. We forgot how easy it was for our parents to make us responsible for things they were legally and morally responsible for, and how easy it was for them to make us feel guilty about that responsibility because we were too young, immature and mentally unable to even attempt to do it. We forgot how difficult it was for us to be a role model for our younger brothers and sisters, like our parents constantly reminded us to be, when we didn't know what a role model was suppose to act like. We forgot how easy it was to learn inappropriate language because our parents were teaching us by using inappropriate language.

We can go on and on, but the general idea is that parents and caretakers were once teens also, and experienced the same type of trials, difficulties and challenges. Although we remember that period, there are many specifics we often suppress, forget and even deny, unaware how important it can be and the difference it can make in truly understanding our youth's challenges today.

Chapter 8

Parents Overcompensating for Their Parents' Efforts/Errors

This is an area that is often associated with attempting to do a better job in raising children than our parents did. Sometimes by correcting what we feel was the wrong way we were raised, we overcompensate in the attempt to make our efforts better. Many of us have gone from one extreme to the other. That is because of some of our parents' efforts in raising us, such as using inappropriate language and many other questionable methods, we become creative in correcting those by using inappropriate ones. We often do not realize the harm we are causing and the long-term effect. Case in point, if our parents were very strict with us and we felt it was wrong, there may be the tendency to be very lenient to a point of allowing our youths to do almost anything they want, or make decision they may not be mentally able to make. If our parents' disciplinary methods were so extreme, we may take a stand to not discipline our children at all, even if it's necessary. If our parents were so authoritarian that we had a fear of expressing ourselves at all, we may allow such a self-expression of our youths that they become disrespectful to us, and to other adults, without interference from us at all. If we were physically abused by our parents, we may take the stand to not only not do any spanking, but not avail ourselves to other disciplinary methods, allowing the youth to grow up undisciplined.

Although there is nothing wrong with having those thoughts of, *When I grow up, I'm not going to treat my children the way I was treated*, the problem is we don't seek alternative appropriate methods to take the place of those we have experienced. Our creative methods become based on those inappropriate or unfair actions our parents took, in turn influencing us to come up with different inappropriate ideas about child rearing because we failed to replace those methods and ideas in our minds. If it's evident our parents' methods did not result in a positive effect with us as adults, the best way to keep us from raising our children the same way would be to seek out and learn a better way to do it and not rely on our own experiences. None of us will be perfect in our parenting styles. However, we can understand and remember what *not* to do, how to prepare, learn and put in practice the suitable things to do with our youths. Overcompensating involves both guilt and lack of experience and information about the situation or situations to be addressed. There is no reason for today's parents and caretakers to fall into this kind of group with the abundance of information that is available to all who have the desire to change those old parental methods and learn new and alternative methods in parenting.

Being in a family that at one time amounted to 8 members, which included only one parent, conflict was not handled very well, especially when that parent, my mother, wasn't there much. There was lots of arguing within the family, and we were not close-knit by any means, except if an outsider was about to harm a family member. Conflict was usually handled by fight or flight and this occurred whether or not my mother was at home. There were times she would physically make us apologize to one another and other times something would be thrown at us by her, like a pot, pan, or anything close she could get her hands on. The handling of discipline was also inconsistent, to say the least. For example, that inconsistency was to the extent where most of the time whatever privileges we lost being on punishment were restored shortly after the incident, mainly because we got on her nerves by being in the house. As teenagers, since we knew the pattern, it didn't bother or deter us from doing things we weren't suppose to do. For us, punishment didn't work.

Male and female roles were defined in regard to the type of housework that person was responsible for doing. Boys did the mopping, washed walls, and were assigned the real physically strenuous work. The girls did the ironing, washed the clothes, and were assigned less physical housework. All of us had scheduled time to wash dishes and participate in cooking meals. Primarily, the environment by way of peers, television and movies defined male and female roles for my brothers and sisters, in addition to those people we observed or chose in the neighborhood that we thought fit the stereotype we felt role models should be. There were really no personal alliances between the family members; we simply had to put up with each other because we had to live together. None of us hung out with each other outside of the house. We all seemed to go in our own directions. We had separate friends and separate hangouts. There wasn't much regard for one another's personal property, or feelings, either. Some of us hid our property, and all of us guarded our feelings. Ethnic traditions were also communicated through the environment by the same means stated earlier for role models. Another way to put it is: "The streets taught us ethnic tradition and value."

Needless to say, it probably would not have been a good idea for me, or anybody, to raise children the same way. I felt, personally, that the best solution was to gather information and learn to better prepare myself for parenthood for an overall positive approach.

Although parents can learn from their experiences while growing up, I again say we should not simply rely on our parents' approach as a style that should be unquestioned and continued to be handed down to our children. On the contrary, it probably won't work, and the resistance from today's youths and teenagers to such methods would be inevitable.

Chapter 9

Mistakes in Raising Children, Youth and Juveniles

Needless to say, parents and caretakers are not perfect by any means, and have and always will make mistakes in raising children. However, there are some areas where parents have control in minimizing not only mistakes, but the very directions children go in. Setting an example is one of the most important mistakes parents make in raising children from toddlers through the adolescent years. Unlike the old days when the expectation of children was to do as they were told and not use the parents' behavior as an example to follow, in today's society, our children will not only do the opposite of what they are told, they will tell that parent about their own inappropriate behavior. As parents, we quite often teach by example, whether we like it or even realize it. Inappropriate behavior, which may seem harmless at the time, always seems to be stored in the youth's memory to be used by them when they grow up. They often apply inappropriate problem solving to the same or similar situations. One good example is:

The parent or parents are at home with the children and the phone rings, or there is a knock on the door. The children are instructed by the parent that if the door is for them, unless it is a specific person the child

39

is told to let in, to tell whoever it is that the parent is not at home, or whatever comes to mind. The children relay what they were told to say, and the person goes away or hangs up.

Regardless of the age of the child, they become aware of a solution that seems to work without much of a problem. Another example is how the parent relates to people around them and relationships. If children observe their parents handling conflict by bad mouthing and violence, if they observe them not talking things out, or trying to find out information involved in conflicts and not looking at all sides to a story before making decisions, it's likely that child will do the same when they become an adult around their children.

Relations are a common ground in teaching children, whether they are taught appropriate or inappropriate behavior. They listen and learn how to manage relationships from us. If the majority of the time they see abuse or toleration of abusive treatment, they are likely to feel this is how a relationship should be. It is the observation of relationships; children become aware of how to handle anger, stress, sorrow, disappointments, joy, responsibility, pain, and various other psychological and emotional survival skills. Therefore, the mistakes we make as parents are handed down or taught to our children. By realizing this fact, before or even during the time we are raising our children, we can take steps to minimize negative behavior we teach by finding positive and more appropriate ways of teaching by example. To do this, we cannot rely on the way we were raised. We need to ask questions, seek answers, and observe related items, books, videos, and people with alternative methods that show positive results. The fact of the matter is we are going to make mistakes. We are also going to be an example, one way or another. That's a given. The key is positively controlling the example we set for the best interest of our children to achieve overall healthy results.

Chapter 10

Do Parents/Adults Listen Enough?

Overall, our youths have a lot to say even when they don't know how to say it, or are unaware what exactly they have said. I would have to say we parents generally don't listen enough.

Many times we are so wrapped up and hung up about what's frustrating about that youth that we miss clues to what they are really saying. Here are some examples of distractions that cause us not to listen well: *Being wrapped up in our life to such an extent we don't have or make time to listen; the child reminds us so much of ourselves or the other parent that we're unable to get past that to recognize the child's own individuality; we're blinded by the love we have for them and they can do no wrong, regardless of what we see and hear, even from the youth themselves; our own impatience; discrimination among one's own children in the household, or playing favorites (it happens).* There are countless things that can prevent us from really hearing what our youths are saying.

Youths often express themselves through their behavior. Because of the rapid hormonal changes they're experiencing, especially during the pre-adolescence and adolescence years, they experience changes they may not only not understand, but may not be able to explain as well. These changes affect their entire body functions, which includes social interactions and understanding themselves and those around them. They may be full of questions, but don't know how to ask them. They may have lots of answers, but may not know how to express them. They may not know how to fit in with their peers, or get away from those peers who they may not want to fit in with or those who don't mean them any good.

It is during these teenage years, as parents, that we need to be very careful and stay alert. It helps to be in tune with the youth to the extent of realizing behavior changes such as sudden defiance or attitude problems. There is much information the parents can get by being as calm as possible and asking questions about the youth's behavior and feelings. Look at how questions are answered through body language and tone of voice to detect clues of what is really meant. Try your best to read between the lines for hidden meanings, unsaid statements, and non-verbal communication. These are important observations. If a child or youth is depressed or suicidal, you would probably need to know how to read between those lines and rely on non-verbal communication to detect those unspoken feelings.

Listening is much more than hearing the words coming out of our youth's mouth. It involves being in tune with them as an individual, looking and listening to their entire body talking to us. From the scratching at the top of their heads, to the tapping of their feet, there are many clues that can be picked up in between. Be aware: Learning to exercise this approach could possibly save many unnecessary problems, even a life.

Chapter 11

Values

Pre-adolescents, adolescents, teenagers, and children in general often relay values some parents may view as comical, at best. However, to them, those values are just as serious as the ones we took years to formulate and establish.

Primarily, we need to understand the so-called value system our teenagers have in order to assist them to be the best they can be. This is an area where we need to think back to when we were teenagers ourselves and try to understand why we did, said and thought the way we did. We all can remember numerous inappropriate, dumb, stupid and ignorant things we did and said. Simply put, during the teenage growth period, the life experience and training is, to say the least, very much incomplete. Youths basically don't have enough life experience to come to any concrete conclusions about anything. However, the mindset is that they think they have, so they show behavior, talk and react as though they do. The kicker is, all parents and caretakers have been in this same category. However, instead of sharing with our children those experiences which may have been associated with those values we had then, we tend to try to forget those times, bury them, and put them in the back of our minds. Some of those experiences may have been unpleasant, horrible, or even embarrassing, but they were experiences that reflected our values and value system at that time. However, quite often we find the need to share that time with our youths only when that child has already crossed the line. We share time when they have already put themselves in situations that are irreversible because of values they have, and because of our failure to identify with them before their misdeed, misconduct, or blunder.

How many of us have sit down and had a warm, heart-to-heart talk with our teenager after something major has happened because of their behavior and shared some similar experience when we were their age. We relayed to them how or what we did at the time, and then our youth asked during our talk, "Why didn't you tell me about this before, Mom (or Dad)."

"I might not have been in this situation."

"I didn't know."

Many times what we try to do is protect our children from going through what we experienced without letting them know what we went through until after they realize what we were trying to protect them from in the first place. By covering up what we remember about the values we had when we were their age, we actually put our youths in a situation where they are guessing about consequences we already know of. They can only guess about why we are doing and saying things to them to prevent them from doing what we did. But it becomes too late, because we tried to protect them without telling them. Then, when we do share that time and those experiences, we realize they understand and can comprehend, whether the subject is about relationships as a teen; trying to fit in, or getting out of trying to fit in because of peer pressure; parental issues; school difficulties; bullies; loner issues as a youth; legal issues; being in the wrong place at the wrong time; youth disappointments; decision making as a youth; or self-image issues, which is a major concern with youths and teenagers worldwide. In essence, if we don't and haven't shared our past, which coincides with their present mindset, we are helping to put our children at risk.

Many of our values today began to develop when we were their age.

If we know, at least from a positive standpoint, that we built our present situation on those past values and experiences, why would we feel we're helping our youths to build theirs by not sharing with them specific experiences before it is too late. In fact, we should make time to share those experiences and values, for no apparent reasons, if just to talk and interact as part of the bonding process. Ideally, it would be a major accomplishment to not only get our youths to understand and remember how our past experiences relate to their present growth period, but to have them to tell themselves that their parents have truly "been there and done that." When they can say this, they are in that mindset to possibly avoid many pitfalls we faced.

Chapter 12

Rules—Peers vs. Family

Many of us parents may not realize how competitive the family or parental rules are with peer rules, and the competition can be brutal, with far-reaching affects. In actuality, it is two different cultures at odds and clashing with each other when it really doesn't have to be. When the parents are aware of this, it could help them realize the mental tug-of-war teenagers may be feeling within themselves.

Some parents may not realize peers of our youths have a very powerful set of rules that, so many times, will and often does override ours. You may recognize or remember some of these:

1. The rule of worrying about what peers think of them, because it is much worse than what the family or parents think.

2. The rule to fit in with peers no matter what they do, or plan on doing, regardless what the parents think about those they are trying to fit in with.

3. The rule to share secrets and problems with peers, because the parents just don't understand.

4. The rule that nothing will happen to them no matter what they do. It's not a chance they will get caught, even though the parents did when they were their age.

5. The rule that they are smarter and the parents dumber.

6. The rule to be argumentative, talk back, and be outright defiant because they don't know any better. The family can't possibly tell them anything.

7. The rule to learn from observing the parents' behavior, not from what they have to give.

8. The rule that it's teenagers against parents/caretakers.

9. The rule of the parents not being fair, regardless how fair they are.

10. The rule that parents will never understand teenagers.

There are many unspoken rules that youths are affected and live by that they are unaware of mentally. However, there are many spoken rules parents expect youths to go by and comply with without so much as an explanation or example, stating the command has been around for ages: "Because I said so." This doesn't seem to motivate compliance anymore with teens. In fact, it doesn't work as much as it used to, even with small children. Furthermore, spanking, slapping, or hitting youths in some states can even land a parent in jail, along with causing overall resentment with the youths involved. In the long run, this causes more harm than good.

Basically, parents just need to understand and be aware; there are some guidelines and rules that youths will bring to the family table. Specifically, those rules are internal, whether they are emotional or psychological, they are real and they are serious. However, they do reflect the growing stage they are going through, and often mirror their peers' growing stage. Parents need to be consistent in being understanding and using awareness. The "I care about you" approach needs to be getting across to youths. Set an example. Be a good listener. Take interest in what they are doing overall.

Chapter 13

How Can Counseling Help?

Many parents have a problem with counseling regarding their youths. However, it can be used as a helpful tool in assisting teenagers and pre-teens going through this growth period. The counseling process does not have to be only when the youth gets in trouble. It can be utilized to avoid problems they could be faced with as well. Parents tend to feel counseling means something is wrong with their youth, or there is a sense of denial. Others may feel they don't need help from anyone and no one is going to tell them how to raise their children. I call this exercising selfish pride, because it doesn't take into account the best interest of the child or children involved. However, since there is no perfect parent, we all can use all the help we can get. It would be a great disservice to our youths not to employ as many positive influences as we can to assist them in developing appropriately and being the best they can be. It should be noted that if juveniles are growing up in ideal situations with both parents in the home, a positive family, and very good environment, they still experience the hormonal changes and the up and down emotional roller coaster they naturally go through. The mental diagnosis of borderline personality is often referring to the juvenile state of mind, because of the difficult changes involved and the rapid personality change the individual goes through. Many of these changes are common, as stated before, even under ideal situations. Therefore, counseling actually should be part of the growing process. We should incorporate it in our parenting, no matter what the style is.

Numerous social service agencies have services for pre-adolescents and adolescents. Just about all those services have some kind of counseling available, just for the asking. This is one area where parents need to put aside pride and denial, and utilize this extra hand and valuable tool in parenting. This would be very instrumental in helping youths to understand themselves, and allowing us to better help them to be the future leaders and productive adults they can and should be.

Chapter 14

Child Development in Schools and How it Could Affect Developing Young Minds

The school system is a vital part of the learning process for our children. Although many school districts in this country have changed with society's growing awareness of our changing society, there's still room for improvement overall. However, there is one area which I feel should be incorporated into the school system in every school district: child development. Considering females are having children at an earlier age and are not educationally prepared to care for them, adjustments need to be made in our society for adequate preparation. The school system appears to be the best place. It appears many of these young mothers simply "wing it," doing so by trial and error rather than practicality. It is felt an excellent time for schools to incorporate this subject into the system would be in the junior high grades, about the age of 12 or 13 years. As English and math subjects are mandatory, so should child development. It would allow the students to not only understand themselves, going through a challenging period in their life, but also allow them to prepare for shaping the future with the children they will have.

It is a reality, and just as important in our society as English and math. It would help developing young minds to make better decisions and set realistic guidelines for the future, regarding the children they will encounter, no matter whose they are. Being taught from the school system would give alternative methods from what the youth does not learn or is exposed to at home. The educational system is already involved in a portion of parenting, in that it teaches disciplines and supervises youths 5 days a week, at least 9 months out of the year. There are many cases where children may see and be around any given teacher in the school system more then a parent of the child who doesn't live in that child's home. Why not include child development within that period the system is involved in from junior high through high school? It should be made mandatory for all students, male and female, to take at least 1 child development class per year until they graduate from high school. This would not only make a difference in results, but approach as well. What do you think?

Chapter 15

The Future Family

The family has always reflected major changes in our social, economic, political and individual lives and we can expect these changes to occur even faster in the future. I think it will affect the behavior patterns of individual parents, whether they are husband and wife or just living together, more than the function of the family itself. Men and women will still come together to fulfill their deep mutual needs for each other, but when changes in our environment occur rapidly, it will make it more difficult to discover who they are and what is needed from each other as parents. Thus, it may put the family system in a position of chaos and confusion.

We need more self-awareness, love, understanding, purpose in life, feelings for our fellow men and women, and a serious approach to family relationships to be injected into a revised and reformed society. Another way of looking at this would be to say that the family is the best of human status and the worst, and it will likely to continue to be. However, its future, in some form or another, is as sure as anything can be and as uncertain as its past. The demands we make of the family will probably never be fully met and will most likely rise, rather than decline, as our standards go up. Youths will continue to disappoint as well as delight parents, regardless of the form of commitments they have, the living style they adapt, or the nature of the relationship they have with the parent.

Our youths need to be taught. Parents need to believe and bring forth the idea that family should be an ever-changing positive learning experience for all family members. Care, love, understanding, cooperation and sharing should be endless experiences. Using these guidelines, it should be possible for youths to take into adulthood some of the following ideas for starting their own families and creating their own positive parenting style.

1. Consult with the other parent on all matters that will affect them and the children involved.

2. Look at the parent/child relationship as a positive learning experience for both the parent and the child and do not take it for granted.

3. Use trust and communications as cornerstones for the relationship and family as a whole.

4. It is not necessary to define roles or tasks in the family using the terms male and female, but recognize and promote femininity and masculinity.

5. Establish a spiritual basis for the family, for assistance in solving problems.

6. Establish a relationship that allows the parent to be a best friend to the child as they reach adolescence.

7. Be able to set aside a special time and place for the family to talk and listen to each other without interruptions or distractions.

8. Be supportive as a parent, but not subordinate to the youths, values or good sense (This does and can happen to parents).

9. Give and receive criticism as an approach to be helpful and supportive. There will be times the parent is wrong. There is nothing wrong with admitting this when the parent knows it, the child knows it.

10. Learn to establish open communication with the children in providing a positive setting for them.

Chapter 16

Checklist and Questions for Guidance

Although there are numerous simple questions to ask, parents may be familiar with some, such as: How was your day? What did you do in school today?

There are other interactions that include asking questions instrumental to creating a lasting bond with our youths. Some of these can be:

Find out what occupation they would like to go into, then find out and get information about that occupation. Discuss it with them and find out what it would take to prepare for and reach it.

Initiate interactions in doing activities with the youth and extend it to doing things outside the home. Go places and take trips together. Invite and take them to the store, laundry, the park, or even take a walk with them. Spend lots of quality time. This involves a commitment that will need to last for years.

You will need to show an interest in what they are doing on an almost daily basis.

Parents can be a friend to their youths and teenagers, but it is not appropriate to expect them to be equal to your status as a parent, nor expect them be your best friend, until they reach adulthood. Until they become adults, the friend aspect is and should be unequal or one-sided.

Get involved with their school projects and homework.

It cannot be overstated that individuals going through pre-adolescence and adolescence need guidance and direction from the parents or parental figures.

Male and female youths both need to learn how to appropriately interact with male and female individuals for a healthy development and balance of relationships. If one of those parents is missing in the child's life, the parent needs to fill that gender role by way of other relatives, whether they be aunts, uncles, grandparents, or godparents. Many times imbalance occurs while the child is growing up because there is no consistent male or female role to follow. Therefore, there is little experience interacting in healthy relationships when they reach adulthood.

Parents often don't realize how much food and beverages affect children. During their growing period, children need numerous nutrients and different amounts than adults need for their proper and healthy development. We buy foods children like instead of what they need. Many of us don't realize many foods that are good for children and have the vitamins and nutrients they need turn out to be things *we* don't like. Also, they may not have tried foods because neither the parent or child has tasted them and they may not be as bad as perceived. In either case, we end up not buying those foods and continue to purchase what's unhealthy. One of the most common beverages bought by parents for their children is soda pop with caffeine in it. We don't realize that quite often this may cause children to be hyperactive, in turn causing them to be diagnosed many times as a hyper child, resulting with being put on medication. Consult your local social service agency to get information about the type of foods and beverages the child should be getting for proper growth. Find out what vitamins are needed and ensure on a daily basis that they get them.

There is no such person who is, or was, born with the natural ability to raise children. Although it may be argued some of us are born with traits that could indicate a special care for children, traits always needs to be refined and built upon with some degree of development. In other words, no one is born with a built-in parental guideline. Although some of us are able to retain information faster and understand information better than others, we all are in some range of learning that information. Hence, we all have to learn how to be an appropriate parent, even if some of us need more assistance than others. We all need help doing it.